AF326798

MIDLIFE MISADVENTURES IN MARGATE

SHE DREAMT OF BARCELONA. HE BOOKED MARGATE

KEVIN J. D. KELLY

CONTENTS

1

BARCELONA, KEVIN. NOT BLOODY MARGATE

My hopes of impressing my potential girlfriend, Sally, evaporated the moment she spotted the hotel. She rolled her eyes. A disastrous sign. *I've lost and John's won*, I thought. I contemplated a U-turn and returning home.

Instead, I accepted my fate, parked my battered and scarred red Mazda across the road in the parking bay, and grabbed the suitcases from the boot. As I lifted Sally's, the weight nearly tore my arm clean out of its socket. "We're only here for the weekend," I said, as the case landed with a thud on the concrete. "I ain't booked a whole week."

A handful of cockney phrases had crept into my vocabulary. Several years ago I'd moved from the north-east of England—Sunderland—to London, and had picked up some of the local lingo. I'd relocated for the love of my life, who'd subsequently broken my heart, but ended up staying in London, where I drifted from relationship to relationship in my doomed mission to meet 'the One'. I hoped I wouldn't end up like Dick Van Dyke in *Mary Poppins*.

I joined Sally in staring at our hotel. On the website, it had been described as beautiful and Edwardian. "Beautiful" was up for debate, but repairs and maintenance had certainly stopped sometime during that era. As we neared the entrance, I spotted an elderly lady hauling her suitcase up, one step at a time. The staircase was long and bumpy, with at least twenty steps. Unable to just stand by and watch her struggle, I dropped our cases at the bottom of the stairs and motioned Sally to wait while I helped the old woman.

"Please, let me get that for you." I held out my hand to grab her case.

"Thank you, young man." She clambered off and left me to haul her suitcase up, one step at a time. I suspected it contained a dead body going by the weight. No wonder she'd been struggling.

When I arrived at the top, the old woman was at the reception desk. I dragged the suitcase the last few yards and deposited it by her side. Then I stood waiting for several moments, expecting to be acknowledged as a chivalrous superhero. Nothing. Not even a well-earned thank you. Unbelievable. I tutted my annoyance and muttered something under my breath about ungrateful old biddies before taking a deep breath and heading back to retrieve our cases.

My heart pumped hard in my chest, and sweat beads were forming alliances and congealing into patches on my forehead. The staircase and overweight suitcase had taken an enormous amount out of me. A reminder I was no spring chicken anymore. And not as fit as I'd once been. Knackered already. Not the greatest start to the trip. Maybe my mate Lesley had been right all along.

"Sorry about that," I said to a waiting Sally, as I reached the bottom of the staircase.

"Sweet of you to help that old lady."

"I don't want to tell tales or make false accusations, but I reckon that case contained her late husband's cadaver. The bag weighed a tonne."

"Aw, you're so chivalrous."

I was about to make another joke, but Sally's face was thunderous. At any minute I expected barbs of lightning to spark from her eyes.

"We need to talk."

"Yes," I said, trying to keep my tone light. "Let's chat after we book in." Stalling for time. I needed to sort out my story. I knew that she was angry about the accommodation, and our trip in general, but I couldn't face her rage and disappointment just yet. In fact, I hoped to avoid "the talk" altogether.

I began the struggle back up the steps, this time with two cases. Sally's was just as heavy as the old woman's.

"Yeah, thanks for helping, Sally," I whispered.

"What's that, darling?"

"Oh, nothing, just catching my breath."

I made a mental note to whisper more quietly. I couldn't have her hearing my true feelings. My self-esteem was low enough already. I had the breakdown of my relationship with Dawn to thank for that, even though we'd been separated for several years already. She'd been the love of my life. I sought solace with her following the breakdown of my marriage a few years before. She'd also manipulated me, gradually chipped away at my wants; and needs to the point where I stopped verbalising any of them. Despite that, I'd wanted to make it work with Dawn. Then there was the betrayal. All my work had been for nought. I'd never recovered from that relationship.

I approached the check-in desk, breathing like one of those perverts who used to phone you up—all deep, excitable breaths. The internet has since made that act of depravity redundant. The reception area and the lobby to the right had an almost *Fawlty Towers* feel about it. It appeared as if someone had found settees of different sizes, shapes, and colours and a mismatched table from the rubbish tip and thought, hey, presto, a hotel waiting area. Not a positive sign. My remaining confidence ebbed away.

Sally's eyes were boring into the back of my head. "Why have you brought me to this dump?"

She didn't even attempt to whisper. I pretended not to have heard. Anything to avoid conflict. "Reservation for Kelly," I barked at the elderly male receptionist, making sure my voice didn't waver, wobble, or just generally give away my anxiety. "Two nights. Thank you."

The man was in his seventies, at least, and had an intelligent face. I wondered whether this had been his job for life or if he'd worked in the City and taken up reception work during his retirement. I often thought about what I would do when I retired, and whether I'd take up another job. Checkout clerk or shelf stacker at the local supermarket, perhaps? Something mind-numbingly boring that would require no thinking on my part, certainly. I wanted to retire from thinking, not just working. Not sure I would do reception work at a hotel. A little too much thought and social interaction for my tastes. He typed in my details on a hidden computer somewhere beneath the desk.

"Mr Kelly." There was a pause as he read his screen. "We don't have a booking for you."

I stared at him for a moment. He was wrong, but I always assume that if someone in an official position tells me I'm wrong, I must be. Even when I know I'm not. I fumbled in my pockets, one after the other, and then held up the proof triumphantly. He gave the booking information I'd printed out a cursory glance. "I'm sorry, but we don't have a booking for you on our system."

"But here. This piece of paper confirms my booking." I jabbed at the piece of paper I handed to him.

He grabbed it and seemed to read every word.

"What are we waiting for?" Sally asked impatiently from the

entrance, arms folded, hip cocked. She pursed her lips and glowered as I looked back at her.

"Everything is fine. It's all good."

It wasn't.

"Hurry up," she said. "I won't allow you or the hotel to treat me this way."

"Won't be long, just a misunderstanding," I said, delivering the words three octaves higher than normal. "I'll sort it out. I promise." My anxiety levels continued to creep up. It appeared as if the weekend might be over before it had even begun.

She shifted her weight to her other hip and tutted. "You better."

The receptionist was speaking to me again. I turned. "Yes, the problem is that you may have booked with this company, but they haven't confirmed with us. Common problem. Happens all the time." He smiled and handed back the paper.

"But what can I do?"

"Are we staying here or what?" Sally demanded.

My heart was beating hard. My hands were damp with perspiration. My belly was playing Twister and losing. "We are," I said, not looking at her. "Just give me a minute to sort it out." My left eye twitched, a sure sign of my state of mind.

"I'm tired and I want to rest. This is outrageous, Kevin. Come on."

"Please, let me deal with it. Won't be long now. One minute."

"You said that a minute ago."

Clearly playing for time wasn't working. "Help me out here, please, I beg you," I said, staring at the receptionist beseechingly.

"Sir, you can either phone the company, or, let me see now . . ." He typed something. "Yes, you're in luck. I have a room free for you to book."

"Book it," Sally said. "Otherwise, I'm leaving. I'll get a train back."

My hands shook as I handed over my credit card.

"Thank you, sir, that'll be four hundred pounds for two nights in our executive suite."

"Wh . . . wha . . . what?" I'd already paid two hundred and fifty pounds for a room. Did I even have any credit left? I gulped twice.

"The only room we have available, I'm afraid."

"I'm leaving," Sally announced.

I whirled around. "No, please wait, we have a room." I turned back to the receptionist. "Yes, that room, please."

My priorities at that moment: stop Sally from leaving, avoid a scene, don't look foolish in front of Sally.

The receptionist took the payment.

* * *

It had all begun a month earlier.

Harry booted the ball. I attempted to dive out of the way but mistimed it, and the full-sized football hit me right between the legs. I collapsed in a heap on the ground. The six-year-old charged towards me and repeatedly kicked the heavy, inflated ball into my body then my head before the object finally flew towards the goal behind me.

From the patio, Sally shouted, "Well done, Harry! You scored a goal!"

We'd been playing for an hour and there was no sign of him letting up or tiring. "Can we rest?" I asked.

"No!"

Well, that was clear enough. I thought about saying something else, but Harry was a miniature tyrant, and I wasn't brave enough to face him or upset his mum, who was keen for me to bond with the little imp.

I threw the football back out to Sally's pride and joy. His inky hair was gelled into a side parting. Despite all his exertions and his clothes looking wrecked, his head was immaculate—not one strand of hair was out of place. He kicked the ball. This time it hit the crossbar then the ground and rolled towards my foot.

"GOAL!"

I thought: *It didn't cross the line. Not a goal.* I said: "Well done, Harry."

"Come on," Sally said. "Time for Kevin to cook our dinner."

"NO!" Harry said. But he followed as I shuffled towards the house.

Sally lived in the part of East London that bordered Essex—a place where residents either told others that they lived in East London or that they lived in Essex, depending on their pride or shame about Essex. A certain reality TV show had divided the natives. This was only my second visit to her home and our second month of dating. I'd yet to stay over, which bothered me. She had made it clear to me that she didn't run to a timetable. Given that I like to know in advance what I'm doing for the week ahead—the month ahead, to be more precise—this was an adjustment.

But now, I was here. In her home. And I was excited to make a great impression on her by way of my culinary skills. I would be making Harry and her the only meal I did with any accomplishment: steak, mushrooms, onion rings, and blue-cheese sauce. My signature dish.

As I stood over the stove in the narrow galley kitchen, Sally squeezed in behind me. Another adjustment. I prefer to cook alone; she insisted on chit-chatting. Multitasking is not one of my strengths. Still, I took a moment to admire her. She was eight years younger than I was and had a shoulder-length blonde bob, a pretty face, full lips, and a fuller figure to match. And at five foot three, she was about four inches shorter than I was. I liked it that way. I was the tallest one in my immediate family.

Sally retrieved a spoon from a drawer and dipped it into the blue-cheese sauce. "This is delicious, darling," she said, savouring the mouthful. "A man with many talents."

Just then Harry ran into the kitchen and screeched to a halt. I fought to contain my frustration. The kitchen was crowded enough already. "Mummy, have you told Kevin about the posh restaurant you went to with John?"

John? Anxiety flipped in my belly. Who the hell was he? And posh restaurant? When?

Sally glared at her son. "Now, Harry. Kevin doesn't want to talk about silly Michelin-starred restaurants and my friend John."

Now it's a Michelin-starred restaurant. My stomach did another somersault. Keeping my eyes on the stove so as not to give away my anxiety, I flipped over the sizzling steaks. "Erm, who's John?" I asked.

"Now, Harry, see what you've done."

I glanced at the boy, who grinned. "He's Mummy's other friend like you." The grin remained. The little monster was obviously trying to get a rise out of me. Had John been here? Stayed over? My anxiety threatened to overwhelm me and turn to anger.

It took an enormous amount of effort to keep a poker face as I met Sally's eye. I cleared my throat. "Oh, well," I said, "a good-looking woman like you will see other men, I guess. I mean, we've only just started dating, and it's kind of my fault we haven't spoken about that yet."

I turned back to the stove to see the blue-cheese sauce rising steadily towards the top of the pan. My cooking was also in danger of bubbling out of control. Panicking, I pushed it off the ring and turned down the heat.

"Yes, darling, that's just it. Nothing to worry about. Now no more chit-chat about John. All right?" Sally grimaced. "Is that sauce burnt? I can smell something burning."

But it was something to worry about. It petrified me. I felt frozen to the spot, unable to think or move, unable to expel breath from my body. A chill ran up and down my back, causing the hairs there to stand on end.

I hated this John, who was suddenly standing in the way of my happiness, making me feel as if I were at the bottom of the food chain. Michelin-starred restaurants? What was that all about? He'd taken her to a fancy restaurant? Well, I'd just have to impress her with a bigger and better act.

My new goal in life was clear: beat John.

* * *

Later that evening, after Harry had gone to bed, Sally and I retreated to the sofa in her lounge, where I broached the subject of spending the night together. I kept one ear trained on the stairs. The last time I'd visited, Harry had been up and down all evening—I swear he did it on purpose to prevent any physical intimacy between his mum and me.

I immediately sensed Sally's defensiveness. Her shoulders hunched slightly, and she sat with one leg swung over the other, facing slightly away from me. Nervousness coursed through my body as I waited for her response. I feared the worst: rejection. It was a familiar fear that had only worsened in the years following my heartbreak with Dawn.

"I want to spend the night with you," Sally finally said, "and my handsome son adores you, but I don't want to rush us. I want our first night together to be special." She angled her body towards me, and I took it as a good sign.

"In that case," I said, "have you got any free weekends coming up?"

She looked thoughtful for a moment. "Well, Harry is with

his dad at the end of the month, but I don't want you popping round here for a quickie," she said, wagging a finger. "I told you at the beginning you'd have to prove yourself and woo me. You agreed to no hook-ups."

I had indeed agreed to this on our first date, two months earlier, at the large Wetherspoons by the river in Camden. We'd met on a dating app and exchanged messages for several days, and I'd made some jokey comments about us being like Romeo and Juliet, given that she came from north of the River Thames and I from south of the River Thames. There was a playfulness to our messages that had attracted me to her—not to mention her physical beauty—so I'd summoned the courage to ask her out and, to my surprise, she'd agreed.

Then, trepidation about the date set in. My recent interactions in the dating world had not gone well. I messaged one woman for ages, and we made many declarations about how we felt about each other only to eventually meet and find there was no chemistry. Zilch. Our attraction hadn't been based on intimacy but on the thrill of sending and receiving messages, which can be very addictive. Then there was the poet who cancelled our date last minute, claiming she had to work overtime, and then deleted me. I mean, how rude?

But the conversation flowed between Sally and me on our date, which was fuelled by alcohol; we spoke about our mutual love of house music, raves, and travel, and I even admitted that as a kid I'd wanted to grow up to be a Jedi Master. She laughed and made a joke about firing up my laser sword. I corrected her and explained it was a lightsaber. There was an awkward silence, which I filled with a question about her last relationship. She explained that her last one, with Harry's father, had ended badly—he'd been an alcoholic, a gambler, and an all-round degenerate. On numerous occasions, she'd bailed him out financially, and by the end of the relationship, she'd spent thousands of pounds on him. I got the impression she'd had a hard life and many problems with men in the past. She'd been clear: she wouldn't put up with any nonsense. This time, she wanted to be treated properly. She wanted to be romanced and wooed for a change. I immediately saw myself as her knight in shining armour, riding in on my trusty white steed to save her (despite the fact that the closest I'd ever been to riding a horse was a donkey ride in Blackpool years ago). Sally knew what she wanted. I liked that about her. And I also sensed a softer side behind her forthrightness, which drew me to her even more.

Afterwards, we went for a Thai meal, and when I walked her to the train station, I told her I fancied her. She smiled sweetly at me. On the Tube, she showed me pictures of her cat, Cecil, and I thought it was sweet how she spoke of her feline with pride and love. Before I jumped off the train at my stop, I told her I wanted to meet again. "We'll see," she'd said with a grin. A few dates later and here we were.

"I want a relationship!" I said defensively. Although I didn't want celibacy either.

"Terrific," she said with a nod. "Then how about you take me away the last weekend of this month?"

I beamed. I'd just got one step closer to beating John. "Okay, great, that would be fantastic. Yeah." Cecil jumped onto the couch and settled between Sally and me. Then he stretched his paw out and placed it on my left thigh, claiming me as his.

"But not just anywhere," she said. "I want somewhere with sun, sea, sand—"

"Sex."

She frowned. "Don't be crude. Sun, sea, sand, culture, heritage, and lovely places to eat where we can sit at dusk and drink expensive champagne."

"I know exactly where you mean," I said, nodding. "Leave the arrangements with me."

I had no clue where she meant.

* * *

Our hotel room was enormous. Bigger than any executive suite I'd ever stayed in. Along with a gigantic bed, it also contained a sitting and dining area. Nineties decor, but not offensively so. I'd stayed in far worse places.

In a former life, I worked as a trade union official and travelled to various left-wing conferences and events in Northern seaside towns. Nowadays, I was far more respectable. I'd sold my soul for a comfortable middle-class existence as a manager of a housing association. In some ways it was like the work I'd done previously, helping, and supporting people, but without the desire to overthrow the government and shout slogans at passers-by while attending demonstrations. I'd slept in various rundown bed-and-breakfasts where the staff were as atrocious as the bedrooms. But as a lefty, I considered it poor form to complain. Even in Scarborough, where the receptionist offered a passable impression of Norman Bates. Rather than object about the strange noises emanating from the kitchen at all hours of the day, my colleagues and I simply went to a different hotel.

Sally sauntered around the space, judging it, taking it all in, her expression blank. *She would make a superb poker player*, I thought. Was she happy or angry? Spotting a row of doors, I moved towards the wardrobe, which looked massive enough to fit Narnia, huge talking lion, and all. I opened the louvre shutters to reveal a kitchenette complete with an ironing board and iron. Surely this would seal the deal with Sally.

"MARGATE?" She spat out the word, and it dripped with sarcasm and disappointment. Frowning in confusion, I twirled around to find her right in front of me, her body inches from mine. Hadn't she hinted at Margate? Sun, sea, sand, and all that? Had I got it that terribly wrong? Again?

I recoiled slightly. "Margate is a brilliant place, with sun, sea, sand, culture, heritage, and some magnificent places to eat, too. All the things you asked for." I backed away and turned my body slightly in defence.

"Heritage? CULTURE?" She moved in front of me again as she spoke, blocking my path of escape. I could turn around again, but I'd be facing the wardrobe.

"Yeah," I said earnestly. "The Turner Contemporary art gallery. And Dreamland is grade II listed. Very posh."

"A fairground. Do I look like a woman who enjoys bloody theme parks?"

I can spot a trick question when I hear one. My heart sank. I had truly missed the target. John was beating me in every way. "No, babe."

"Don't 'babe' me. This is a dump?"

Sally worked in business development in banking, and her career was important to her. I thought perhaps it gave her security in a way that her past relationships hadn't. Often she'd work late and sometimes at weekends. She was clear about her ambition. The job paid her well, and she'd got used to living the high life. I questioned whether my finances—or, more accurately, my credit card—could match this.

"Where did you want to go then?" I blurted, feeling more and more out of my depth.

"I've told you countless times that you need to woo me, make me feel special. Why on earth did you pick Margate?"

"Because . . . Because . . . Because . . ." I gathered myself as best as I could. "I thought this ticked all your boxes and I'm wrong and for that I'm sorry."

I went to take hold of her hand so she could see my sincerity, but she jerked her body away and sniffled. "I thought you would be different, that you would get me. But you don't. At all. I wanted you to choose a city with a beach, by the sea, with sun and culture and heritage seeping out of every orifice. Barcelona, Kevin. Not bloody Margate."

I saw my future unravelling before my eyes as Sally moved further away from me and emitted a couple more sniffles. She was the one. I wanted a relationship with her. Needed it, in fact.

Stupid fucking waiter. It was all his fault.

* * *

"Tell me about this mystery woman in your life," my friend Lesley asked me. He and I were catching up at a Mexican restaurant near Liverpool Street Station, a halfway point for us—Lesley lived in north and I in south-east London, and every so often we'd meet up for dinner. We rarely contacted each other in-between, choosing occasional physical catch-ups as the basis for our relationship. In my message arranging the mate date, I'd told him there was a new woman in my life. His reply was to ask what had happened to the other woman.

We were about the same age, but he had a thin, stretched out, wiry body and didn't carry any excess, unlike me. He was touchy about the spelling of his name, and refused to acknowledge he had the girl's spelling. He should have been Leslie not Lesley. His idea of fun was running marathons. We'd met at a party thrown by one of my exes three years ago, and we'd bonded over football. He was a Manchester United fan, whereas I supported Everton. Both of us had a pathological hatred of Liverpool. Our biggest fear: Liverpool winning a trophy. A fear that multiplied as time went on and they got better.

I need your help, mate," I said, ignoring his question. "Where shall I take Sally?"

"Aha. So, she has a name." He smiled and looked thoughtful. "Have you asked her where she wants to go?"

"Yes and no," I explained her criteria. "But she wants me to choose. It's a test to see how well I understand her." I felt like a stranded teen in a dystopian future, trapped in a series of increasingly gruelling tests.

Lesley stared at me and cocked his head. "How long you been dating?"

I told him it had been about two months. "But she's also seeing this other bloke, John, who took her to a Michelin-starred restaurant the other week. Show-off." I scratched my head and let out a deep sigh.

"You only finished with what's-her-name two months ago. What was her name?"

"That's irrelevant," I said, pouring water into our tumblers. "Where am I going to take Sally?"

"What's important is that you jump from one relationship into another. Why?" He raised an eyebrow and paused for effect. "Another question for you—what's it like when you're single?"

I loved Lesley to bits, and he was one of my best friends, but he fancied himself as an amateur counsellor and I was never in the mood for counselling, least of all from a novice one. He continued. "What emotions come up for you when you're not in a relationship?" He leaned in closer and his gaze intensified.

Persistent little bugger. "Depression. Sadness. Emptiness. Happy now? More importantly, where should I take Sally? She's the one. I feel it in my bones."

"Hang on a minute." Lesley frowned. "I thought what's-her-name was the one. What was her name?"

"No, she wasn't." I shook my head and took a sip of water. "I had to end it."

"What happened?" He lowered his eyebrows.

Nosy sod. "That doesn't matter. Listen, mate, you're not helping at all. Where am I going to take Sally?"

The waiter interrupted our conversation. Despite our living in the twenty-first century, he appeared to be a Victorian gentleman, given the style of his ginger beard and moustache. He wore ankle-length jeans, no socks, slip-on shoes, and a plaid shirt. Definitely a hipster. "Are you ready to order your food?"

Lesley said that he was.

"Can you give us a few more minutes?" I said. "Actually," I held up my hand to stop him. "Before you go. My friend here is being useless and unhelpful. Where would you take a girlfriend on a trip to impress her? She wants sun, sea, sand, culture. Any ideas?"

"Hmm." He pursed his lips. His moustache gained volume and threatened to envelop his mouth. "Well, you could do worse than a jaunt to Margate. I live there. It has all that, plus it's trendy." The lips reappeared, having escaped the bristly ginger hair.

"Really? What, the arts? Things to do? Restaurants?"

He nodded. "There's the Turner art gallery. Well worth a visit. Dreamland is a heritage site now. There are loads of places to eat. Yeah. Take her. Very popular nowadays."

"Margate? That's an inspired choice, mate. Superb. She'll love the place. I'll take her on one of the scary rides so she clings to me. Margate it is then."

All my problems evaporated like mist on a summer's morning.

"Jane!" Lesley proudly announced. "That was her name." He raised his glass and clinked mine. "Margate though, mate? Really?"

* * *

In the days that followed my decision, doubts about the whole adventure set in. Lesley was of no help. He sent me messages telling me that I should slow down with Sally and not rush into another relationship and that he thought Margate was a terrible idea. He even told me not to go, claiming no one in their right mind would take their potential love interest to

Margate. Other than the terrible advice, this was unlike Lesley. We never messaged like this in-between our meetups. But what did he know? Okay, he was in a loving marriage to the woman of his dreams and from the outside, they looked like the perfect couple, with their own interests as well as each other. But besides all that, what did he really know about successful relationships?

Wanting the trip to be memorable, I attempted to reserve a prestigious five-star boutique guest house, but it had no rooms available. I soon found that most places had no rooms available. My panic increased with each rejection. I was that drunk bloke in a club just before chucking-out time. Desperate. And so, I lowered my expectations and booked a three-star hotel with a 3.5 rating on TripAdvisor on the edge of Margate in a place called Cliftonville, which sounded like an imaginary town from *The Simpsons* rather than a romantic place for lovers.

When I read through the reviews, "adequate" and "average" came up several times. Who wants adequate or average? These are two of the most offensive terms in the English language. The booking was a monumental risk. I rarely booked anywhere without a rock-solid 4.5 on TripAdvisor. A 4 was perilous. A 3.5 was tantamount to juggling unpinned grenades.

As I worried about the booking, another worry raised its head, so to speak. I wanted sex, lots of it, to be on the agenda for Margate, but I'd had problems in that department in the past. Sometimes, my soldier didn't want to salute. The thought of my difficulty made the issue worse. Talking to Sally about my quandary was out of the question. Doing so could ruin the potential relationship. And Margate had to be perfect. What to do and whom to turn to?

At the end of my tether, I did what any normal human being would do: I researched erectile dysfunction on the internet. Amongst all the adverts for magic potions, the dodgy videos, and the magical blue pills, there he stood, a hero of mine, showing me the way, telling me the solution.

I clicked on the video, and the greatest footballer of all time convinced me it was all going to be fine and persuaded me to seek advice from my doctor. When I was young, every boy I knew wanted to grow up to be Pelé. He'd scored a thousand goals in his career. Who was I to argue with him?

I booked a GP consultation.

* * *

"So, Mr Kelly, what seems to be the problem?"

One issue Pelé had not addressed: what if your doctor is a woman? I'd forgotten to insist on a male physician when making my appointment. Caught between a rock and a hard place (perhaps not the best metaphor, considering my circumstances). I had to choose: the humiliation of not being able to perform on my weekend away with Sally, or the shame of speaking to a female GP about my problem. This problem hit against my feelings about being a man. Real men, I'd always thought, get it up and satisfy their woman every time. I didn't . . . on both counts. Therefore, I was less of a man. Talking to anyone, let alone a woman, only compounded my shame and anxiety around the issue.

"Take your time," the doctor said, glancing at the clock.

"Yeah . . . so . . . I, erm . . . I've started a . . . you know . . . with a woman . . . and so the issue is . . ."

"You want to have a check-up. Book it with a local sexual health clinic. Is that all?"

No, not at all.

I thought of the emptiness I felt whenever I was single and mustered my composure and as much mental strength as I could. "The thing is, I've started a new relationship, and in the past, I've suffered from not achieving an erection, or if I do, it not staying erect."

I impressed myself with my boldness.

"Well," she said, not missing a beat, "I would also advise you to have a full sexual health check-up. In terms of your erectile dysfunction, I have some questions I need to ask you."

By the end of the appointment, she'd prescribed me sildenafil—in other words, Viagra. "Take the pill about an hour before sex and two hours after food," she said. "And avoid alcohol when taking the medication."

With that obstacle under my belt, no pun intended, I just had to seduce Sally and all would be perfect in the world.

Right?

2

ROMANTIC MEAL AND MONEY TROUBLES

Sally was sitting on the end of the bed, peering at me. "Tell me you've at least booked a decent meal for tonight." She tilted her head and raised both eyebrows.

"Of course." I gulped. The room's phone rang. *Saved by the bell.*

"Mr Kelly," the voice on the other end said. "It's George from reception. My apologies, you were right—you did reserve a room for two nights. We'll sort the issue out and refund you, so you're not paying for two rooms."

I knew it. Both relief and indignation coursed through me. "Absolutely no problem. I'll come down straight away."

"No need, later will be fine."

"I'll come down now." Really, I just needed some breathing room to arrange dinner plans.

I hung up and pretended to be annoyed. "Sorry, Sally, I need to pop down to reception and sort out my card, as they've charged me twice. Then I'll tell you all about the fantastic restaurant we're eating in tonight."

Once I'd left the room, I opened my mobile trying to search

for restaurants. But the internet on my phone wasn't working, and neither was the hotel's Wi-Fi.

"I am so sorry for the mix-up, Mr Kelly," said the receptionist, as I reached the desk.

"It's okay." It wasn't. I'd known I was right. But at least I'd get a refund.

"I have refunded the money back to the card you used earlier. This means you can stay in the executive suite for the price of a regular room."

The least they could do. "Thank you," I said, switching my phone off, hoping a reboot would help. "So I'll receive the cash back straight away?" I switched it on again. It took an eternity to come to life.

"I am afraid the repayment will take three to five working days, sir."

Amazing how money can leave your account in a matter of seconds but getting it back in takes the dreaded "three to five working days." Thieving, robbing . . . "Urgh."

"My sincere apologies if that is a difficulty for you, sir."

"Oh. No. My mobile. It's so slow." I held the phone up and shook it, thinking that would fix things. My stress levels continued to rise. "If I left now, would I receive my money back?"

"I am afraid not, sir. You have booked in and paid for your room, and your payment is non-refundable. Is there a problem with the suite?"

"No. It's fine. But my girlfriend thought I was taking her to Barcelona, and it doesn't impress her one iota we're in Margate." I shook my phone again. "And if I'm being honest, the hotel is a little downmarket for her sensitivities. We may not be together for long." I stared at the mobile, willing it to switch on. "And now my stupid mobile has stopped working and I require a top-notch restaurant. She thinks I have a reservation."

"Why is she under that impression, sir?"

"Erm, well, because I told her that. This is turning into a disaster. URGH." My phone screen was still blank. I heaved a sigh then unloaded my story onto the poor sap.

"I quite understand, sir," he said, once I'd finished. "My wife would much rather go to Barcelona. But we have sun, sea, sand, culture—"

"Exactly. But she hates this place."

"Well, Margate is not to everybody's tastes, I'll grant you that, sir. But perhaps I can help with your restaurant booking?"

Another wave of relief washed over me, and I ventured a half-smile. "Really, you would do that? You can do that? That would be fantastic. Thank you."

"Well, let me try. There's an establishment I can recommend, which overlooks the beach and the sea. This time of year, and with the weather today, you will likely see a wonderful sunset. And the food is exquisite." He paused. "I'm guessing you need the reservation for tonight?"

"Yeah, please, this evening. Otherwise, I'm in bigger trouble."

"Give me a minute, sir." The receptionist picked up a landline and I left him to it. Sort of. I tried to listen in, but he covered his mouth and the mouthpiece, so I overheard only occasional words.

"I know."

"I realise that."

"Appreciate your help."

"Okay then."

As he hung up, I checked his face for clues. He was inscrutable.

"Fantastic news, sir. I have secured you a table for two. I will write the name and address of the restaurant for you. Now, the booking is at 6.15 and you will need to vacate about 8.15. But the reservation is on the terrace, so you'll get to experience the beautiful sunset."

I formed a fist with my right hand and shook it jubilantly. "Fantastic news! Thank you." Perhaps the weekend wouldn't be a disaster after all. *Yeah, John, you've not won yet. Kevin is back in the game.* "What do I owe you?" I fumbled in my pockets and found nothing but fluff.

"Nothing, sir. I hope you have a wonderful time tonight with your girlfriend and leave an extra tip at the restaurant as a thank you to them."

"I'm so grateful. Much obliged. Gracias."

I glanced at my phone, which was finally working again. 4.30. Plenty of time.

* * *

Back in the room, I found Sally still on the end of the bed, arms folded, frowning. "What took you? You were ages."

"Sorry, I sorted out the repayment on my card. Three to five working days to go back in my account though. Robbing—"

"Where are we eating tonight? It better be amazing."

I smiled proudly. Finally, I had a win to share. "We're dining on the terrace of one of the premier restaurants in Margate. We'll be watching the sun set over the sea. Romantic, hey?"

She softened. "Oh okay, that sounds idyllic." She paused. "Though not quite Barcelona."

"It will be intimate. And all on me. You won't have to pay a penny."

She pursed her lips. "Oh, sounds better and better. I like the sound of this." Then she smiled—her first smile of the trip. My stomach did two flips in response.

Unlike Sally, who had a beautiful beam, I had a crooked grin, which I was self-conscious about. I tried not to smile too much, which wasn't that difficult for me. I was born with a cleft palate (but not a cleft lip). You couldn't tell by looking at me except for the twisted teeth, nose, and lack of a defined chin. The main physical impediments: I couldn't blow up balloons, play the trumpet, or pronounce *th*. The sound always came out as *d*. So "the", "this", and "that" were "de", "dis" and "dat".

I sat down on the bed beside her, picked up one of her hands, gazed into her eyes, and said, "I will give you one of the most memorable weekends of your life."

Sally cupped my face with her other hand and eyeballed me. "You better." Then she glanced at her watch. "What time is dinner?"

"We need to be at the restaurant by 6.15."

Gone was the softness. "What? I can't be ready that quick. When were you going to tell me about the time of the booking?"

"I'm telling you now. The best establishment in Margate and we're on the terrace."

"Kevin, Kevin, Kevin." She jumped up and headed to the bathroom, shaking her head, which then did that exorcist thing, turning around while her neck stayed still. "You need to wash down while I'm showering because there won't be time for both of us to shower."

Yes, she was bossy. But I figured I needed that in my life. Left to my own devices, I was directionless, barely capable of looking after myself. I was certain that part of filling the void my failed marriage had left inside me meant finding a woman to tell me what to do and when.

* * *

We exited the hotel at 6.00.

"You look stunning, Sally," I said, gazing at her appreciatively. I loved having her on my arm. Her being a bit of a looker certainly reflected well on me.

"How long to the restaurant?" she asked. It was a frequent conversation between us. It always made me think of a five-year-old asking "Are we there yet?"

I called on Google maps and its intrusive spy satellites. Three minutes. That couldn't be right. I quickly realised the calculation denoted driving time. I changed the mode of transport to walking. Sixteen minutes.

"Ten minutes."

I surveyed our surroundings and concluded we were in a rough part of town. That, and my desire to get to the restaurant on time, led me to quicken our pace. But Sally tugged back on my hand, like a dog owner pulling back on an overexuberant puppy. So, of course, we walked at Sally's speed.

As we approached Margate's central area, vintage and hipster shops materialised. Soon, we came upon the Turner Contemporary art gallery, situated right next to the harbour. It comprised two futuristic buildings with sloping roofs. I thought it would fit in on the set of *Alien*. It seemed to symbolise the struggle taking place between the working-class natives and the marauding middle classes seeking to take the heart and soul of Margate for themselves: the building drew middle-class visitors to what had been a working-class seaside resort. The gallery represented the present and future and the resort the past.

I'd learned that the gallery commemorated the artist Joseph Mallord William Turner, who painted landscapes, often marine ones, and I shared this with Sally. His most famous painting was *The Fighting Temeraire*. He'd gone to school locally and visited the town regularly throughout his life. I'd always been interested in art, but the research I'd done beforehand was for Sally's benefit, not mine. Impressing her was at the top of my agenda.

As I took in my surroundings, it became clear why the waiter who'd given me terrible advice loved Margate. There were hipsters everywhere. I tended to dislike hipsters. I mean, what did they stand for? They said they were rebelling against a consumerist society yet wore expensive designer clothes and typed away on their overpriced MacBooks while drinking craft beer—all funded by their rich parents, no doubt.

And what is it with their beards?

And why are they so skinny?

And why do they insist on wearing glasses, even if they don't need them?

Ever spotted a clean-looking hipster? Neither have I.

At least hippies stood for something.

We passed some steps leading down to the beach. On them sat a bearded bloke who looked like an American Civil War veteran typing away on his MacBook. Typical. Further down on the steps was a small group of women wearing clothing from the shops we'd passed. They were all drinking what I imagined to be expensive lattes, the clue being their frothy lips; I didn't imagine they'd succumbed to rabies. Close to them was what appeared to be a vast family gathering. The kids ran riot while the mums and dads smoked ciggies and drank cans of lager.

It seemed Margate attracted two types: white working-class people (chavs) looking for a traditional seaside resort and hipster refugees from East London searching for somewhere cheaper than London.

I embodied both. I'd come from a working-class background but currently lived a middle-class lifestyle. The late afternoon or early evening meal was now not "tea" but "dinner." A source of shame for my family, who now viewed me as a soft, Southern shite, who ate dinners, not teas. My accent had also softened over the years. My deep baritone held a hint of the Liverpudlian lilt, but you had to listen carefully to spot it.

In the 1960s, Margate was a battleground between mods and rockers, but by the 1980s, skinheads had supplanted the rockers. In the 2010s, the battle was between the hipsters and the chavs, with the mods nowhere to be seen. As far as I was aware, the most violent stand-off involved the occasional frown, tut, or whispered insult. Possibly the mods will return, and the working and middle classes will unite to fight their common enemy.

I checked my phone. The time was 6.20. We were already late for our reservation.

We wandered past a fish and chip shop, or "chippy", according to my Northern upbringing. A small child suddenly sprinted out of it.

"Septimius!" a woman shouted after him. Or perhaps it's spelt "Septimus." He was either named after a Roman emperor or a Transformer.

"SEPTIMIUS!"

Darling little brat face ignored his mummy and darted into the road. I grabbed him by the waist as best I could, swung him around, and planted him back on the pavement right in front of his mum. I was a superhero. Yet, the language that came out of his mouth as I plonked him back down would have made a docker blush.

"Septimius, never run off like that. What have I told you?" Then his mum looked at me. "And you! How dare you touch my son!"

I couldn't hide my shock. I mean, I'd saved the kid's life. Was I to get no thanks for my heroics?

She repeated herself for the benefit of the growing crowd. "How DARE you TOUCH my SON!"

Not only was I not a hero, now I was apparently a pervert or a celebrity from the 1970s. Eyes were looking at me from every direction, judging me. Sally tugged on my jacket, trying to pull me away from the scene. I took her hint. Embarrassing her was the last thing I wanted to do.

As we hurried away, the woman continued her rant. "Did YOU witness THAT man touch MY child?"

I turned to Sally, seeking affirmation for my heroism.

She shook her head. "Septimius? Who names their child Septimius?"

Point for Sally.

We finally arrived at the restaurant. The time was 6.31.

* * *

As we waited to be greeted, I chewed on a nail, sure we'd missed our booking. Sally slapped my hand away. Restaurants, particularly the more upmarket ones, were often sticklers for punctuality, at least in my experience, but I tried to exude confidence as a hostess approached.

"Good evening, sir, do you have a reservation?"

"Yes, table for two, the name's Kelly."

"Let me check." She looked down at the clipboard she held then squinted at me and smiled. "I just need to speak to my manager. I'll return to you shortly."

She headed to the back and stopped to talk to a tall man wearing black trousers and a white shirt with the top two buttons undone. He spoke animatedly while pointing a finger at a clock on the wall, gesturing to us, and shaking his head. Not a promising sign. My tummy did flips that had nothing to do with how beautiful Sally looked.

The hostess returned. "Thank you for your patience," she said with a smile. "Because you were late, we have given your table to another couple. If you had phoned, we might have been able to keep it for you."

A crushing blow. I was hungry. And I'd promised Sally the most memorable weekend of her life. Perhaps it would be, but for the wrong reasons. I opened my mouth, ready to beg and plead, but before I could speak, Sally held up a forefinger.

"We have a table booked," she said, her tone harsh. "Are you telling me that because we were one minute late you gave our table away? Not good enough. I demand to speak to your manager. Immediately." She folded her arms and her gaze darted towards the back of the room.

Inwardly, I winced, praying she would shut up. I hated scenes, and she was about to make a massive one.

"Actually," the hostess said, her smile now gone, "you were sixteen minutes overdue. As I said, if you had rung, we might have been able to keep your table reserved."

"Not interested. Fetch the person in charge. Now."

"I'll check if he's free." She forced a half-smile and turned on her heel.

As soon as the hostess had left, Sally faced me. "You need to be more assertive, Kevin, otherwise these people will push you around. I want my table on the terrace with the sunset, and if you can't sort this out, I'll do it myself, like I always do."

Saved by the manager. As the man the hostess had been talking to earlier approached, Sally transformed into another woman. "Hi, darling, thank you for coming over. I appreciate you taking time out." She stroked his arm. "Do you work out? Wow, you must do. Your muscles are so defined under your shirt."

He smiled and gulped twice. She pressed on. "Today is our tenth wedding anniversary, and it would *devastate* me not to have our meal here. Please, can you sort it?" She stroked his arm again and fluttered her eyelashes.

He cleared his throat. "I am sorry, madam, but there is nothing I can do other than offer you a table inside. I'll send the hostess back to get you sorted." And with that, he turned and walked away.

This would utterly wreck the weekend. I could feel Sally seething beside me. Mustering my courage, I gave her a look that I hoped conveyed *I've got this* and then hurried after the manager.

He stopped as I caught his arm. "I'm so sorry," I said. "I appreciate you're only doing what is right and following the rules. But please, how about we start in the bar and when a table becomes free we move outdoors? It would mean the world to my girl—my wife."

He eyed me suspiciously. *I've blown it*, I thought. I reached into my pocket and pulled out two twenties and a tenner. I gave him one of the twenties. He looked at the note in his hand then at me. Then he stared pointedly at the remaining money in my hand.

I gawped and shot a glance at Sally. Her arms were crossed, and she was tapping her foot, watching the exchange. I immediately gave him the additional thirty pounds.

"Have your starter and drinks at a table inside, and at 7.15, I'll find you one outside on the terrace."

"Thank you ever so much. You're a star."

I shook his hand and went back to Sally.

"Well?"

Palms out towards Sally, I cocked my head and spoke softly, hoping to conciliate her. "Well, we'll start here and he'll find us a table outdoors from 7.15."

She huffed. "I want to be on the terrace now." She waved her hand in that direction then stamped a foot on the ground. "Why did you make us late with that stupid child?" she said, her tone holding no forgiveness. "I hope you told the manager how crap he and his restaurant are."

I didn't. That wasn't my style.

"Yes, I did. Come on, let's sit down and order our starters, and I'll also request an ice-cold bottle of champagne."

"Pink?"

"If that's what you want, yes."

She almost squealed. "You're the best. You're almost forgiven."

We sat down at the bar and then, like a massive show-off, I ordered pink bubbly. Painting the town red is all well and fine, but splashing the town sparkly pink works just as well—for Sally, anyway. Thankfully, it appeased her.

"My ex never stood up for me, or us," she said, slurping her bubbly. "Annoyed the hell out of me."

I topped up her glass. "I'm not your ex, I'm Kevin, and I'll always stand up for you and us." I knocked back my drink and refilled my glass as well.

"You know," she said, "at work, I don't take any crap from anyone. I know what I want and I get it. I want you to be like that." I nodded, and my finger automatically went to my mouth. Sally slapped it away. "Don't bite your nails. Filthy habit. Plus, it makes you look weak."

"Sorry, I know, bad habit." I sat on my hands.

"I want my man to be assertive and know what he wants," Sally continued. "Do you get me?"

She studied my face, which I kept expressionless. It was something I did when I was annoyed—a defence mechanism I'd learned when I was younger. Finally, I said, "You had a horrible time with your ex—the drinking, gambling. You always had to sort him and his problems out. I'm not that man. I know what I want, and I want you." I took a gulp of my drink.

She kept staring at me, seemed about to say something, turned away and gathered her thoughts, then gazed at me again. "I can't go through what I went through last time again. It almost broke me. Affected my job, too. Poor Harry and I vowed never to allow a man to place me in that position again." She finished off her second glass, and I poured the rest of the bubbly in.

Taking a deep breath, steeling myself for a moment of intimacy and connection, I took her hand in mine. "Babe, you are an amazing woman, a fantastic mother, and you deserve the absolute best in life. That's what I want to give you."

Sally beamed and swigged her bubbly, her eyes on me. I silently breathed a sigh of relief.

"What do you fancy next?" I asked, seeing as we'd demolished the bottle.

"Besides you, darling? Surprise me."

My prospects were looking up. Sally had relaxed and was even flirting with me. I touched the magic pill in my pocket, the one that would hopefully allow Captain Kelly to lift off.

I called the bartender over. "Two strawberry daiquiris."

"Oh, I love cocktails," Sally gushed. "Especially daiquiris. You *do* get me."

I was destined to drink not-so-manly drinks. I accepted my fate. As we waited, our drinks arrived and I checked my phone. 7.16. I caught the manager's eye across the room and he held up two fingers. I hoped it meant that our table would be ready in a couple of minutes and that he wasn't offensively indicating I go away.

Sally also glanced at her mobile. "Why are we not on the terrace yet? Where is that manager? Fetch him over. Are you going to let him get away with this?"

Thankfully, as though sensing the chaos that was about to ensue, the man approached us. "Mr and Mrs Kelly, your table outside is ready."

"Oh, we're not married." The alcohol had blunted my brain, and I'd forgotten our earlier lie.

"You wish," Sally said, elbowing me. She smiled at the manager. "Bottle of bubbly and he forgets our marriage. Wishful thinking, I reckon."

As soon as the manager looked away, she shot me a look as if to say *shut your mouth, you idiot*.

I complied.

The terrace was small but bustling, and they sat us sideways to the setting sun. The ball of fire looked orange and hung low in the sky over the sea, bathing us with its dwindling heat and adding a spark of romance. Fuelled by alcohol and a desire to impress Sally further, I ordered an expensive bottle of Rioja. She loved red wine. Rioja in particular.

"Aw, lovely, darling, you remembered my favourite. Shame we're not drinking it in Barcelona. But this is beautiful, though. Me, you, an amazing restaurant, and the setting sun. Thank you."

Sally reached over and squeezed my hands. I grinned at her. The more she drank, the softer—or at least less hard-edged—and flirtier she became. *This might be the solution*, I thought, only half-jokingly. *Keep her in a state of constant inebriation.* Not something you'd read in a self-help book on relationships.

Still, I fancied her. I loved her directness. She would make me a better man and fill that void. This would have to trump the fact that sometimes she said and did things that made me uncomfortable.

* * *

The food arrived. I'd ordered steak, Sally mussels.

"Here, try one," she said, holding the creature out to me.

I'd never had a mussel. I didn't mind prawns or white fish, but I disliked all other seafood. "What do they taste like?" I asked.

"The sea. And it will slide down your throat."

I almost gagged in response. Who wants to eat the sea? Not me. "Wow, that beautiful sunset, hey," I said, shifting her focus away from me and escaping her desire to force-feed me the disgusting vagina of the sea. The sun was now lighting the clouds and sky with reddish hues. "Gorgeous. Just like you."

She gazed at the sky for a few seconds and then shifted her attention to my face. "We need to change your hairstyle. And those black glasses are too severe on your face."

I shifted in my seat. Dawn had been the last woman to try to change me, to the point where she chose all my clothes and wouldn't talk to me for hours if I ever bought any without her. I shuddered at the memory. *But Sally isn't Dawn*, I thought. *She's different. I think.* I stroked my head. "I've been wearing my hair like this for fifteen years." Then I fiddled with my spectacles. "But I'm due an eye test, so some fancy ones would be agreeable, I guess."

She pursed her lips and continued looking at me. "I don't think red is your colour."

I smoothed down my shirt and started biting my nail. "Really? I love this top."

Sally took my finger out of my mouth. "Don't do that. You're like a baby." I smiled, gulping at air. "You need a woman's touch to help you take better care of yourself and have more pride in your appearance."

I felt as if I were on one of those reality programmes where they strip people of their clothes and self-esteem then remake them. I thought I had brilliant dress sense, but I suppos Sally understood style more than I did and her telling me what to wear was acceptable.

Divorce, redundancy, lost friendships, broken relationships, heartbreak, and many terrible decisions over the years had taken their toll on my confidence. I needed to get this right with Sally. Dawn had broken more than my heart. For a while, I felt as if she'd broken me. In many ways, I'd never fully recovered. And so, if being fixed meant changing my hairstyle, glasses, and clothes, so be it. I was up for that.

I decided to let Sally's comments wash over me and focus on the delicious food and even more sumptuous Rioja. For the first time that weekend, I settled in and enjoyed the moment. Soon, my insides felt warm and fuzzy, although it could have been all the alcohol swilling around my body. And the lust.

Once our plates had been cleared away, I ordered us coffee and Baileys, wanting to prolong the moment—what better way than with a decadent and potentially liver-failure-inducing coffee? Then, remembering my pill, I slipped to the toilet to take the tablet. An image of the doctor flashed into my head. *Avoid alcohol when taking the medication*, she'd said. What did she know? *I'll be fine.*

Time passed; the sun well and truly set. When the bill arrived, I gulped and did a quick calculation, at first believing the total was a mistake. But what could I expect after a two-course meal and enough drinks to satisfy a Roman Bacchanalia? I put on a brave face, asked for the card machine, and even stuck on a decent-sized tip.

"Excuse me, sir," the waiter said, as I pulled on my jacket. "There appears to be a problem with your payment."

"Oh, dear." I frowned. "I put in the wrong number." That didn't surprise me, given the amount I'd drunk that evening. Every time I closed my eyes, the world spun a little quicker on its axis.

"No, sir, your card has been declined."

"What? No, it can't be . . ."

Visions flashed through my mind. The card. The hotel. Three to five business days. I recovered quickly. "Not a problem, I have my other one." At least I thought I did. I rummaged frantically in my pockets. Then another vision. My card in the pocket of my other jacket. *Shit!* I'd left it in the room. Guess I was paying with cash. A final vision: bribing the manager for the table with fifty pounds.

Heat rose from my neck into my face, and I took several gulps of air. I shook my head. I couldn't believe I wasn't able to pay the bill. The shame of it. I inhaled deeply, needing to ask the dreaded question.

"Sally, I'm so sorry, erm, do you have any money or a card on you? I'll transfer payment straight away."

"What happened to 'you won't have to pay a penny?'"

"And you won't, darling, I'll pay you back. Remember about the—"

"Don't bother." She took the machine and paid the bill. I averted my eyes, thinking that maybe if I wasn't witnessing the scene, it wasn't happening, while inwardly berating myself for being an idiot and forgetting my other card.

I tried to hand over a bunch of crumpled notes. "Here's some—"

"Put that away," she whispered, her tone dangerous. "You're making a show of yourself and me."

"I'm sorry, I'll pay you back. I'll transfer it right now." Except my phone was dead.

"John hasn't made me pay for a single thing. I'm so disappointed."

She'd hit below the belt, cutting me right to my core. Shame, anger, and fear fought for possession of my body. Fear won, but only just.

I ran after Sally as she marched away, receipt in hand.

3

I DON'T EAT FRUIT

I woke up the next morning with a fuzzy head and fragments of memories: Lots of alcohol. The beautiful sunset. The bill. My card being declined. Chasing after Sally. Standing in the bathroom looking down at my old fellow, demanding he stands to attention. Him refusing. Maybe alcohol and the pill didn't mix after all. I groaned and rubbed my hand over my face.

The shower was on in the bathroom. Then, silence. Moments later, Sally appeared in the doorway with one towel wrapped around her body and another around her head.

"Morning," I said sheepishly. "I'm sorry about last night. Tell me how much I owe you. I'll transfer the money over to you." At least my phone was charged.

"You look like shit."

As I propped myself up in bed, a shooting pain pierced me behind my eyes. "About last night—"

"You embarrassed me. You spoilt a lovely evening. Kevin, you're a grown man. You should be able to take me out without incidents like that. I want a man, not a man-child."

"Yeah, you're right." I felt like curling up into a ball to avoid the verbal blows that both she and my mind were throwing at me.

"Don't patronise me either. The receipt is on my bedside cabinet. Transfer the money." She went back into the bathroom.

My hands shook. I didn't know if it was because of the alcohol or the confrontation. She was right. Time to grow up. How difficult was it to whisk away the woman who was nearly my girlfriend for a weekend without drama or incidents? I shouldn't be blaming the hipster waiter for suggesting Margate, or the hotel for charging me twice for the room. I needed to change. I needed to take responsibility.

But I recalled several of the uncomfortable feelings that had crept up yesterday. I was putting in a lot of time, effort, and money to make Sally like me. Yes, I'd made mistakes, but my heart was in the right place. So far, the trip had been all about treating her and giving her a weekend she would remember. What about me? I deserved a fantastic weekend too. What I'd been doing so far certainly hadn't worked. And I didn't want to see more similarities between this relationship and my relationship with Dawn. I promised to share more of myself with Sally, let her get to know more of the real me.

Today would be different. I had cash. I had my other card. I would get my shit together and make sure Sally and I both had the most memorable trip ever.

As I got out of bed, I scanned the room and shook my head. We'd been in the space less than twenty-four hours, but Sally's belongings were scattered everywhere. She was one of the messiest people I knew, but only in the bedroom. Her room was reminiscent of a bomb site. I once nearly suffocated when my legs got caught up in a pair of tights and I fell head first into a mound of her knickers, stockings, and bras. I managed to extract myself before my oxygen expired. Imagine the coroner's report.

But the rest of her house was tidy. I'd already received instructions on how to load a dishwasher the proper way. She stored spices, sauces, and dressings in a way that escaped me. I had put them away incorrectly on more than one occasion. For the most part, she'd bring order and organised condiments into my chaotic life. We'd figure out the bedroom later.

My tummy grumbled. First, I needed to work out where to take us today.

* * *

Over breakfast in the hotel's restaurant, we met a group of people who'd been extras in *One Flew Over the Cuckoo's Nest*. Mercifully, this broke the tension between Sally and me and saved us from the forced pleasantries we'd been exchanging. Then we bonded over observing and gossiping about our fellow guests. There was an elderly couple accompanied by a man I presumed was their son. Then there was a duo about my age, both obese, wearing brightly coloured shell suits. A pair of middle-aged yoga instructors said grace before tucking in. An interesting assortment, to be sure.

The breakfast was incredible—a full English, which included bacon, sausage, Heinz baked beans (surprising for an establishment of this ilk, but welcome), eggs, mushrooms, and black pudding. The fatty nourishment did a decent job of soaking up all the excess alcohol swilling around my system.

Sally leaned on her arms on the table and gazed at me. "I'm going to have some fruit," Sally said. "Do you want some too?"

Warning bells sounded in my head. I hated fruit. *Do I tell her or lie?* I remembered my earlier promise to myself to be more open with her. "I don't eat fruit. Thank you."

Sally's arms almost collapsed from under her. "You don't eat fruit? But everybody eats fruit."

"Well, not everybody," I said, a knot forming in my stomach.

Revealing any little thing about myself was jarring. "Not me. I don't. Hate the stuff. Never liked it. Never will."

"Seriously? No fruit?" She stared at me, shaking her head, a confused look on her face.

"None."

"Why?"

"I just despise it—the texture, everything about it." I shifted uncomfortably in my seat.

"What, so you dislike apples?"

"Yes."

Sally's mouth dropped open. "Bananas?"

"I refer you to my previous answer." My little finger went to my mouth. I chewed, watched as Sally's gaze shifted to the offending nail, and then pulled it away and sat on that hand.

"Oranges?"

"I refer you to my previous answer for all forms of fruit."

"But how can you say 'texture' when they all have different textures? That can't be right. There must be some you like. What about yoghurt or juice?"

"Smooth ones, great. Any bits, no." I waited patiently for the onslaught of questions to cease.

"Hang on, so you like those things, but not fruit itself? So, you like the flavour?"

"I like them if there are no pieces."

"What about ice cream?"

"Again, I love fruit-flavoured ice cream, but no lumps."

"That is the weirdest thing ever."

The knot tightened again. I didn't want her to think I was weird. "Makes perfect sense to me. I've just never liked fruit. I'm an adult now, so I choose not to eat the disguting objects." I started to relax. This was me. This was my truth.

"That doesn't sound like an adult choice to me."

Oh, hang on, was she insinuating that I was a man-child again? The same uncomfortable feelings I'd experienced over dinner the previous night came rushing back. In fairness to Sally, I'd had the same conversation over the years with every ex-girlfriend, and with friends and family. They all thought it was peculiar too. Was I odd? Seemed perfectly sensible to me. The knot disappeared. Point for Kevin.

While Sally went to fetch her fruit, I collared a waiter, a simple-looking, callow lad. "Are there any pleasant places nearby for a day out?" I asked. Sally had asked me this morning where we were going. I'd lied and told her it was a surprise.

He scratched his head, his chin, and finally his nose—inside. "Ramsgate is a good day out, or Broadstairs, although there is less happening. More for older people, your age."

"Thank you." *Cheeky sod.* Ramsgate sounded preferable. But what would Sally choose? *Forget that. I'll choose.* Plus, I remembered, it was supposed to be a surprise.

When she returned, I confidently informed her of the plan.

Margate had not yet been lucky for me. If someone had asked me at that moment, I would have described it as a quintessentially English seaside resort full of drunken, working-class men and women wearing "kiss me quick" hats, sporting sunburnt faces, and holding a dribbling ice-cream cone in one hand and a half-empty can of Stella in the other. And worse: hipsters. No, Ramsgate had to be a better bet. Ramsgate would be my gateway to Sally's heart.

"Ramsgate?" she said, lifting an eyebrow.

"Yeah, Ramsgate."

"Are you sure? I thought it was for old people?"

"No. For our age. Let's go there. I want to."

Okay. Ramsgate it is."

* * *

As I drove us out to Ramsgate, Sally asked me what I knew about the place. I had researched it quickly, while she was getting ready, so I had some facts with which to dazzle her.

"Interestingly, they started building Ramsgate Harbour in 1749 and it wasn't finished until 1850."

"You are a mine of useless information, aren't you?"

I chuckled. "I reckon the builders were paid by the day—101 years to stretch out a building job?"

"That's taking the piss," she said, nodding. "My ex was a builder. He would do something like that."

I'd also learned that the harbour was famous for being the only "Royal Harbour" in the United Kingdom. On arriving, I could see why the kings and queens had stuck to their parks and palaces over the years. The beach wasn't as sandy or as tempting as Margate's. The town centre cried out for renovation or tender loving care or something. It was all quite depressing, to be honest. I needed to stop seeking the advice of waiters, hipster or not. But I reminded myself I had money and both bank cards. Today would be better.

While not hot, the weather was warm enough to be at the seaside. I found a fantastic spot near the harbour wall, away from the crowds and shielded from the wind, and rented two deck chairs. Once settled, I slapped on plenty of sun cream. I burn as easily as freckled ginger men do. I am neither but do sport a pallid complexion most of the time.

"Put some on your bald spots, darling?"

"What bald spots?" I patted my head gingerly, genuinely confused.

"Ha-ha, funny. Here, I'll rub some on your head." Sally massaged cream into the crown of my head then finished on the sides.

I frowned. "Am I a baldy?"

"Well, kind of. The hair is a lot thinner round the spot."

"How enormous is the bare part?"

She pressed a forefinger and thumb together then pulled them two inches apart.

"That big?"

She nodded.

News to me. How could I not have known this? I'd been living under the misconception that I owned a full head of hair. Sure, I might have admitted to the thinning out and receding of my fringe over the years. But now, the incontrovertible evidence was that I was balding. Well, if nothing else, her rubbing cream on my bald patch showed that she cared about me. That was a wonderful thing, yeah? I needed a woman in my life to tell me the truth—even when the truth was unpalatable.

Both relaxed, we slipped into friendly chat and banter. She even complimented me on the spot I'd chosen. I felt good about my decision to visit Ramsgate. Spending time together was what this weekend was all about, and that's exactly what we were doing. We spent the morning soaking up the sun. She read the *Daily Mail* while I read the *Guardian.*

In today's polarised times, being on opposite ends of the political spectrum might spell a relationship doomed to failure, but other things were more important to me. We also had dissimilar interests in films, books, and TV. I loved watching Stanley Kubrick films or losing myself in my fantasy of becoming a Jedi Master in science-fiction films. She preferred romantic comedies. Surely this must be at least one film we both loved together? But we both appreciated the same kinds of music and middle-aged raving. We both liked home cooking, as long as I was the chef, and going out to eat and drink. I wanted a woman to take care of me. She wanted a man to love her. We were perfect together.

After a takeaway lunch of fish and chips, a lunchtime mainstay for English seaside resorts, tiredness overcame me. *A nice brief nap will be just the ticket*, I thought, closing my eyes.

* * *

Next minute, Sally was shaking me. "Babes, did you put any more cream on? Because you are burnt."

Groggily, I prised my eyes open. "Yeah, no, well, earlier, when we first arrived, but not since. How long have I been asleep?"

"We must have both nodded off. At least two hours or more."

Crap. That was way too long for my skin to be in the sun without cream. I'd burnt in far less time in the past. Feeling suddenly panicky, I touched my face and quickly snatched my hand away. My skin was hot and tight, as though it had been stretched over a fatter version of my face. Meanwhile, the sun shone at full blast. Not a cloud in the sky.

I grimaced and looked at her. "How do I look?"

She smiled weakly. "You need to check yourself in a mirror. You're a bit red."

We decided to retire to a nearby bar. While Sally grabbed a table outside, I headed to the toilet to assess the damage and found a mirror in which to gawk at myself. Staring back was a red panda, giant white patches around its eyes and all, thanks to my sunglasses. Not a look I would recommend. Would Sally not fancy me anymore? Would I get sunstroke? So much for a perfect day.

As I walked back to the table, Sally stared at me, open-mouthed, but then laughed in a half-sympathetic way. "*A bit red*, you said." I flopped into the chair across from her. "Look at me. I look ridiculous."

She giggled. I sighed then couldn't help but chuckle too. Her laughter had eased my tension. Better she laughed than recoiled in horror.

Despite my overheated face, we enjoyed a couple of hours of people-watching and taking the piss out of passers-by. I relaxed again, the vibe between us light-hearted. The alcohol might have helped.

"Jesus," Sally said quietly, as a woman walked by. She took a sip of her beer. "Did you see how short her skirt was? Not an attractive style with her legs."

"God, she has a face like a slapped arse." Hypocritical of me, of course. I was the one who had the face like a slapped arse. I glugged back some beer, enjoying the icy coldness of it against my parched throat.

As two young women sat down at a table to the right of me, I clocked them, but in my peripheral vision. They stood out from the crowd. Long legs, high clunky heels. One had tattoos running up the side of her left calf, the other over her exposed shoulders and back. Given their 1950s-style hair and outfits, I wondered if they were burlesque dancers.

Sally interrupted my concentration, saying something. *Crap, what did she say?* Her glass was empty. Did she want another drink?

Luckily, before I could ask her if she did, she repeated herself. "Shall we pay up and head back, darling?"

"Yeah, yeah, sounds good."

She narrowed her eyes. "I know you were ogling them, hussies."

I made a snap decision to forge ahead with the theme of honesty. "Yes, I may have been looking, but that was all. I'm here with you and you're the only one for me."

"Erm, okay. I guess. What can I expect? You're a man."

"Exactly."

I checked her face for anger, disappointment, annoyance—but she just smiled briefly and picked up her phone.

I poked the tablet in my pocket then popped it in my mouth while Sally was engrossed in her mobile. Once again, things were looking up.

* * *

We arrived back at our hotel room to find that the housekeeper hadn't visited. Quickly feeling overwhelmed by the mess and wanting it dealt with, I rang reception. A woman greeted me on the other end of the line.

"Oh, hi, yeah, this is Kevin Kelly, in room 35. Housekeeping hasn't been to our room today. Can you sort that out? Please."

"I'll investigate it," she said, sounding weary.

"Thank you, that would be great."

Sally suddenly appeared right in front of me, inches away. "Are they sending someone, honey?" She moved closer. I closed the gap between us, wrapping my arm around her waist. She wiggled her eyebrows, giving me the impression that perhaps, romance, and physical intimacy was on the cards.

"Yeah, they are." I pulled her in a little tighter.

"When, darling?" She backed away from me, holding my gaze, annoyance flickered in her eyes.

"Soon. Imminently." I shook my head, exasperated by her being on my case.

"Hmm, shame."

Damn, had I missed an opportunity here? I sidestepped her and moved to one of the enormous bay windows. Across the road, a wedding ceremony was taking place on a raised wooden platform. A plastic gazebo provided cover. Surrounding the platform was a large group of smartly dressed people of all ages.

I pointed this out to Sally.

"I want to get married on a white tropical beach in the Caribbean," she said, coming up beside me and looking out the window. "While the sun is going down. And I want a big, sparkly antique diamond engagement ring and a platinum wedding band on my finger."

I tried to hide my shock. Yes, I'd known she wanted to

marry again, but the specific details meant that she'd put a lot of thought into it. And why was she telling me about them? Was a promise to marry her part of my wooing? A worrying turn of events. Experience had shown that I didn't suit marriage (although I had my two fantastic sons). Commitment and a long-term relationship? Yes, I wanted them, no question about it. A marriage? No.

After a long-term relationship, you can walk away from each other and be left to deal with only emotional distress in the aftermath. Divorce, on the other hand, presents many legal processes and battles that serve to compound this emotional distress. Another big difference is that in a divorce, you must legally assign blame—who's divorcing who and for what reasons—and then split the assets. Although any kind of breakup is emotionally painful, give me a splitting up after a long-term relationship any day of the week. Lawyers get a hell of a lot richer with divorces than splits.

Trying to work out how much Sally's fantasy wedding would come to, I counted on my fingers. Not subtly enough.

"I hope you're not counting the cost? *If*—and this is a big if —we become a couple, you'll want to wed me one day, right? You want me to be happy, don't you?"

A trick question? I mean when you're with someone, of course, you want to make them happy. In a relationship, I never set out to make the other person unhappy, although I could appreciate that I usually ended up doing just that.

"Yes, I want you to be joyous," I said with a smile, attempting to sidestep the marriage interrogation.

Sally stared at me with a frown on her face. "*If*—again, this is a big if—we start a relationship, eventually you would love marriage, wouldn't you, handsome? And a wedding on a beautiful beach in the Caribbean?"

Her use of the word "handsome" was my weakness, and she knew it.

"Maybe." It was only a half-lie—I imagined us on a beautiful beach in the Caribbean. We could deal with the whole wedding thing later. The clock was ticking, and the weekend was half over. Time to make my move.

Literally.

"WOAH there, tiger, what are you doing?" Sally said while backing away from my approach.

"Nothing, why?" I said, as innocently as I could.

"Come on, honey, you have that stare in your eyes."

I frowned. "What stare in my eyes?"

"Your 'I want sex' stare."

"A gaze of affection, I'm sure."

"No, it was certainly your 'I want sex' stare. And is that a wonderful idea when housekeeping is due any minute?"

"Erm, well, yes, terrible timing now, honey," I said, regretting phoning housekeeping. I'd shot myself in the foot with that one. I also made a mental note to check out my sex eyes. Clearly, they needed work.

"Margate, drinks, nothing too heavy?" I asked. My stomach still churned and my head still ached from the night before. I didn't think I could cope with another piss-up. And despite my failed attempt, seduction was still on my mind.

"Sounds perfect."

* * *

The lights of the Margate Harbour Arm—the part of the pier from which the lighthouse jutted out—sparkled, illuminating the calm sea. We walked along the road leading from the Turner gallery and past the lighthouse. Up ahead were several pubs and restaurants. So, like moths to light, or drunks to pubs, we headed to the brightness.

We stopped outside a small restaurant with a rustic, kitchen-type vibe about it. Brickwork and bunting adorned the interior, along with electric-blue cupboards. Huge chalkboards listing the specials dominated the far wall. "How about here?" I asked. "Seems like our kind of place."

On our second date, we'd enjoyed a meal at a similarly rustic restaurant along London's South Bank. We'd then visited the Tate Modern, walked along the river, and then shared our first kiss while a group of young lads cheered and jeered. We'd blushed and snuggled into each other. There's something about a first kiss—will there be that chemistry, that physical attraction? And how good will it be? After our kiss, my worries about those things had faded. So had Sally's.

A waitress approached, and I pointed to a table outside, as the evening was balmy. She cleared the table, and we sat down.

"Wow," said Sally, smiling appreciatively. "What a beautiful view, darling."

It really was. From our vantage point, we could see Margate, the Harbour Arm, the lighthouse, and a glimpse of the gallery. Straight ahead was the beach and the sea. "Two glasses of Rioja, please," I said to the waitress.

"A bottle of house red is the same price."

I glanced at Sally, and she nodded. Who doesn't love a bargain? And it was only half a bottle of wine each. We'd be fine. "A bottle of house red, then."

We also ordered some food and then ate and drank—slowly in my case—and observed the world as it passed by. Voices carried across the beach. The Harbour Arm was a hive of activity, with couples and families parading up and down it.

"This place reminds me of that restaurant we went to on our second date." I sipped a little red wine. "Do you remember?"

"Oh yeah," Sally said, nibbling on some bread. "And here we are by water again. Such a lovely day."

"Except for that film we watched at the Tate, by that artist about 'that time of the month' though." I forked a couple of garlic mushrooms in my mouth and immediately regretted it. I tried to smell my own breath by cupping a hand to my face.

Sally half-smiled. "What are you doing?"

"Oh, nothing." I blushed. Not that Sally could tell as my sunburnt red face disguised it. "What was that film we watched?"

"Oh yeah, about menstruation." She shook her head and peered at me. "You walked out because you felt nauseous."

"No, I didn't." I sat up straight and puffed my chest out. "Just not my cup of tea. That's all. That wasn't art."

"Remember what happened by the river?" She grinned.

"Of course." I raised my eyebrows and paused for effect. "You snogged me."

"I did not!" She slapped my arm playfully. "If anything, you pounced on me."

"How dare you," I said with mock indignation.

"Such a lovely moment though, our first kiss."

"Shame about the audience," I said with a chuckle. "Fancy jeering us." Then I gazed right at Sally. "I thought it was a fantastic first kiss." Butterflies fluttered in my belly, and I felt the same connection to Sally I had on those early dates.

Soon, I'd finished my garlic mushrooms, with no obvious effect on my breath; Sally's plate of prawns lay empty.

"One more for the road?" Sally asked.

"That would be lovely."

I signalled to the waitress. "Two glasses of red wine, please."

"Another bottle of house red?"

I made eye contact with Sally. I was fine, a little tipsy, but didn't want another bottle.

"Yes, please," Sally said, turning to the waitress. "That would be fabulous." I pursed my lips and blew air through them. *Don't get inebriated*, I told myself. I still had plans to seduce her.

As we sipped our second bottle, I relished the romantic

ambience and how connected Sally and I seemed to be. But in the back of my mind, John still loomed, and I knew that until he was out of the picture, I'd never relax. Now or never. I grabbed Sally's hands and held them in mine. "I know this isn't the weekend you wanted, but today has been special, aside from my sunburn and checking out those 'hussies'." I chuckled. "I've loved this evening with you."

"You're right," she said, reaching up to stroke my face. "Tonight has been fab. You're lovely."

"I like you, Sally, I do. You're beautiful, smart, you take care of me, and I have fun with you." Nerves kicked in and my legs shook a little. Tonight was the night and I wanted it to be perfect for her and me. I imagined us both together in bed and my leg shook harder. I took a deep breath, to calm myself.

"Aw, that's sweet. You're adorable."

"I'm glad we've had this time alone. It's brought us closer together."

"Yeah, you're right, Kevin. Today has been special."

"I think we have a future side by side. I do. I'm not seeing anyone else and have no plans to. I only want to be with you. I want us to be a couple."

"Are you asking me to be your girlfriend?"

"Yeah, I guess I am. Yeah, I am. Will you be my girlfriend?"

"Well, I still haven't made my mind up about you or John yet. I want to make the right decision."

I swallowed the lump that formed at the mention of his name and fought to remain optimistic. "Is that a yes then?" I said jokingly.

"No. Maybe. Perhaps. Still early days, yet."

"Not a no?" Always the optimist unless I'm being a pessimist. I squeezed Sally's hand and beamed. She smiled back. "Shall we go back to the hotel?" I asked.

"Yes, let's do that." *Is she thinking about what I'm thinking? Is 'back to the hotel' a euphemism for sex?* I studied her closely. Were her eyes 'sex eyes'? The light was dim, so hard to tell.

"You're doing that eye thing again." She smirked.

Crap. "No, just adoration, that's all."

"Oh, I'm not against it. In fact, well, let's get back to the hotel."

Get in! She'd had on her sex eyes after all.

Loud voices and thumping music flowed out of the pub next door, where it appeared there was a party in full swing. Sally glanced at the pub then looked at me and laughed. "Next door first?"

In the dark, it was difficult to suss out how serious she was being. "Nah, come on, let's go back," I said with a cheeky wink, which probably came across like a nervous twitch. I fingered the pill in my pocket. Tonight was the night.

4

WEDDING CRASHERS

Back at the hotel, the wedding reception we'd seen earlier was in full swing, and the divide between the hotel lobby and the reception room was non-existent. Abba's *"Dancing Queen"* blasted through the speakers.

"Oh my god," Sally said, tugging on my hand. "I love this song! Let's dance?"

I groaned internally. "Shouldn't we go to our room—and to bed?"

"Oh, come on. We won't stay long, I promise. Come on! 'Dancing Queen'!"

I wasn't ready to share my lack of coordination with Sally yet, and my mind was on a dance of a more private nature. But she pulled me towards the noise, despite the minor matter of our not being invited. Alcohol and self-doubt had drowned out my newfound bravery and my conscience. The drinks were flowing. The trepidation and anxiety in my stomach were bubbling.

Just as we entered the reception room, *"Dancing Queen"* stopped. "Aw, that's a shame," Sally said. "Shall we have a drink? Just one, heh?" She plonked herself in a chair at an empty table.

The tablecloths were white, and the space was adorned with blue and pink balloons and decorations, along with the tacky *Congratulations on Your Wedding* banners one might find in a cheap card shop. On the table were those annoying pink confetti hearts. An arrangement of white, blue, and pink plastic flowers sat in the middle of the table. Cheap and nasty.

Poor bastards, I thought. They didn't know what they were getting themselves into. At first, it would be all "I love yous" and walks along the promenade and afternoon sex. Before they knew it, they'd be having a full-blown row over whose turn it was to dust the ornaments in the front room and fighting—through solicitors—for ownership of the music collection and access rights to the dog. *Enjoy it while it lasts.*

It was clear Sally had no intention of moving any time soon. But no one had stopped us from coming in. Tacit agreement that we were welcome to stay, right?

Just one more beverage, I told myself, and then I'd whisk Sally to our room for a night of seduction. I thought of the blue pill in my pocket. *Crap. I should have taken it by now.*

"Two large vodka and Cokes," Sally said, indicating I should head to the bar. "Diet, though, no getting fat. Or *fatter*, hey."

Ouch. That one hurt a little. Okay, so I carried a stone or two extra, but I wasn't obese. If I lost a little weight, would that improve my chances with her? I could feel my confidence ebbing away. Still, I popped the blue pill into my mouth as I walked to the bar.

While I waited for our drinks, my doubts about crashing the wedding returned. In my head, a debate raged. One voice told me I was wrong—the bride and groom had paid for their party and here I was, drinking for free. *Where's your card and present for the newlyweds? What if they beat you up out of revenge?*

They could be gangsters, and before you know it, you're in the boot of a car being driven to an anonymous industrial estate. Worse than that, what if the irate couple humiliates you? That one hit home for my anxiety. All the while, another voice, slurring his words, told me everything was fine, everybody seemed chill with our being here. *Stop worrying. Just avoid all contact with the bride and groom, don't talk to anyone else, and don't draw attention to yourself. One more drink and then back to your room.*

The drinks quickly disappeared once I returned to the table.

"One more for the road?" Sally said, setting down her glass.

That sounded familiar. "Same again?" My heart wasn't in it, but the alcohol had prevented me from coming up with any bright ideas of how to get us out of there.

"Yeah, and easy on the Diet Coke this time. We don't want to suffocate the vodka, do we?"

"No. We don't want that."

One more drink and then bed.

* * *

Where the hell is she? I was back at the table with our drinks, but my date was nowhere to be found. I scanned the room . . .

There! There she was, being led towards a photo area—of sorts—by a bloke who I assumed was the official wedding photographer. My powers of deduction were not failing me (the huge telescopic camera hung around his neck gave him away), although my voice, legs, and eyes were. He and Sally skipped through a cardboard archway with flowers around the edge. Tackiest reception ever, yet here I was.

Noticing the photographer giggling away with her, I raced over, suddenly insecure, and jealous. I grabbed Sally's hand and planted a quick peck on her cheek. Then I smiled at the photographer. If this had been a jungle, I would have roared at him, marked my territory, and mounted Sally. But this wasn't a jungle. A peck on the cheek would have to suffice.

I passed a drink to Sally, who immediately downed half of it. I followed suit. If you can't beat them, join them, hey? Unfazed, the lensman guided us to a treasure box full of blow-up plastic props. Sally chose a guitar; I picked up a massive plastic sword. I hoped he understood the dual symbolism. The sword was about two feet long. I may have been overcompensating.

"CHEESE!" the photographer said.

Our cue to pose. We posed. Our photo was taken, and then the photographer handed me a card with a website address and login details, presumably so I could access the photos. I had no interest in seeing them. I'm not a great collector of photos.

Sally finished her drink. I followed suit, seeing this as a cue for us to retire to our room. "One more?" She hiccupped.

"Bed?" I tentatively countered.

"No, one more and then bed. Go on."

As I made my way to the bar, I thanked God for the chairs to keep me steady. Everything was spinning. At the counter, I caught sight of my reflection in the mirror behind the bar. I didn't recognise that man. All I could see was a drunken, wedding-crashing slob. I averted my gaze. The critical voice in my head berated me for my appearance and for forgetting all I'd vowed earlier about getting my shit together. Not for the first time, I'd let myself down. Why did I find it so difficult to follow through on promises to myself?

Then, on my circuitous route back to the table, unsteady on my feet, I came upon the most wondrous sight ever, and for a moment, life was good. *Oh my god.* An entire table full of sweets! Flying saucers, jelly babies, jelly beans, dolly mixture, cola bottles, taffy, double lollies, fizzers, and candy hearts (to name more than a few). All my favourite ones from childhood. I was in sweets heaven.

"Sally. 'Ere. Come here."

As she stumbled towards me, I staggered to meet her, but a small child stepped in front of me. *Don't touch the child! Remember what happened last time.* Certainly didn't want any more accusations flying around. I avoided him, holding my hands up in the air—"See not touching him!"—and unceremoniously bumped into a table. A drink then spilt its contents on the table's two occupants. The man whispered something to the woman.

Sally stopped in her tracks and stood unsteadily, facing them. "Hey . . . HEY! Yes, you! What the fuck did you just say? Say that to my face?"

The man glanced at the woman, who rolled her eyes.

I wondered what John would do in this situation. "Woah," I said. "Don't you . . . don't do that. That . . . rolling your eyes thing." My rivalry with John fuelled my temporary bravery, but the aggression was certainly unlike me.

The woman smirked at me. I dislike being smirked at. I find it offensive, even when I'm sober. I stepped forward to give them a piece of my alcohol-addled mind, stumbled, steadied my balance, pointed my finger at them, opened my mouth, then shut it again.

Words failed me. Where was Sally?

Aha, at the sweets table. I weaved over to her, somehow not getting punched or encountering any other small children or spillages in the process. There were small bags and fat, greedy, enormous ones. My choice was clear. "Sweets. Sally. SWEETS."

On our way back to our table, Sally snatched a tacky wooden— or maybe it was plastic—heart with "Kell and William" inscribed in the middle. We sat down to feed on our bounty.

"Them over there?" Sally said, gesturing with her head. "Him and his smirking missus, yeah, been giving me eye rolls, just cos you knocked into their table. The cheek of them rolling their eyes at us. Who do they think they are, rolling their eyes at us? Have I told you? Them over there, mister and missus eye rolls. I'll tell them what I think of them."

"No, don't do that. Don't want any trouble."

"Such a scaredy-cat, aren't you?"

"No, let's find the happy couple," I said, my judgement diminishing rapidly. "Let's tell them about it. They'll sort it out." I tried to spot Kell or William but couldn't focus. The room was spinning faster by the minute. That should have been my cue to leave. That and the fact that I was getting embroiled in confrontations—something I never would have contemplated sober.

"Sally, Sally, see them over, them over there . . ."

"Over there?"

"What?"

"You said see them over there."

"Who?"

I finally spotted the bride and groom, sitting across the room from us. I waved. "HEY!" Then I noticed that the smirking woman was talking to them. As she left, the now unhappy-looking couple turned to stare at Sally and me before engaging in an intense conversation.

I smiled and gesticulated at them again. They glared at us and then at each other and shook their heads. "A shame, just married and arguing already," I said. See, I knew marriage was a terrible idea.

"Who?"

"What?"

"Just married and arguing already?"

"I don't . . . oh yeah. What's with their faces, the couple who got married. Over there."

"Argh, that is a pity."

At that moment, I realised I didn't like the music; the party needed something to revitalise it. I stood up and momentarily forgot why. Quickly remembering, I made my way to the DJ but couldn't see any records or CDs, just a laptop. How times have changed.

"Hey, mate," I said, leaning in close. "You need to liven this place up. Dead in here. How about a bit of the Prodigy?"

He shook his head.

"Go on, put on a bit of '*Smack My Bitch Up*'. You'll lift the fucking roof off this place!"

My inebriation was clear. I'd both approached a DJ and believed that "*Smack My Bitch Up*" was appropriate for a wedding disco with small children.

He shook his head again and pointed me away. I walked back to our table, also shaking my head. Once again, no Sally. Through my wavering vision, I spotted her at the bar talking to a barman. *Jesus, I can't leave her for a second.*

Before I could process what was happening, Sally was back at the table, the barman hovering close behind. "They're chucking us out! Apparently, this is a private party." Her face was furious, and she had a hand on her left hip and waved her right one as she spoke.

"Please," the barman said. "If you'd like to follow me. I'm sorry for any misunderstanding. I can serve you both drinks in the hotel lobby area. On the house." And just like that, he removed us from the wedding reception with minimum fuss and the power of complimentary vodka—after Sally had gathered up our booty, of course.

As soon as we were settled in the lobby, I swigged down my final vodka and Diet Coke of the evening. By this time, I'd lost my sense of taste, along with my common sense. And every other sense. I'd been hurled out of a few places in my day, and each occurrence had involved alcohol. Once, I'd picked up a large potted plant, gripped the flowers, and then spun the pot around above my head, like a knock-off Morrissey. I was seventeen, in a pub in New Brighton. Youthful exuberance. But getting thrown out of a wedding? At my age?

This was a first. Where had I gone wrong?

5

THROBBING HEAD AND TOE

I woke up first this time. My head was banging. The events of the previous evening crept back into my head one by one, and each revelation made me wince.

Here we were. I'd whisked Sally away to woo her, seduce her, and make her my girlfriend. Failure on all three fronts.

She let out a little snore. I needed to rouse her. The pill I'd taken the previous night was still working its magic. When we finally got back to the room, I'd headed into the bathroom to wash then sneaked towards the bed only to find Sally zonked out. My plans for seduction had been thwarted.

But not now. All systems go. Captain Kelly was ready for action. I was shocked but delighted by this turn of events. The evidence was there for me to see. But I had to make it appear to Sally as if she'd woken up naturally. Perhaps it was courage that gave me the impetus to begin Operation Wake Up Sally, or maybe I was still inebriated from the evening before. I'll never know.

First, a short coughing fit.

I checked for any signs of life. Nothing. It had to be a gradual awakening, not a heart-attack-inducing wake-up call.

I got up. Knocked my leg gently against the bed three times.

Nothing.

Maybe bathroom activity will help. I left the door half open and peed. Not the easiest thing to do in my excited state. Two thunderous farts ripped from my body. My first of the day are usually booming. They didn't disappoint on that front. Only afterwards did I consider the fact that being awoken by breaking wind might have been a turn-off for her. When I ran the taps to wash my hands, I turned them on full blast. Next, it was time for my early-morning nose-blowing. My foghorns blared out. Also not the most romantic sound, but better than a fart, surely.

Exiting the bathroom with a smile, I found Sally still fast asleep. I threw my arms in the air, exasperated. What the hell did I need to do? Clambering back into bed, I bounced once and lay on my back, waiting. Nothing. I shoved myself into her back, spooning her. Nothing. I got out of bed and returned to the bathroom to brush my teeth.

And then, as I wandered back into the bedroom, she was stirring. Taken off guard, I panicked and ran around the bed, wanting to be there in pole position, ready to seduce her as she woke. Instead, I stubbed my toe.

Screaming loudly, I launched forwards into a chair, banged my head on the top of it, and half knocked myself out.

Next thing I knew, Sally stood over me, looking concerned. "Are you okay, darling? What happened? Oh, that is a nasty bump and bruise on your head."

I lifted my finger to my head and prodded the sore spot halfway between my right eye and my hairline. A sharp, shooting pain pierced my head. "Ow! That's sore as hell." I tried to stand. My little toe throbbed. "OUCH. God, that hurt."

"What the hell happened? I heard an almighty clatter and a thud and when I checked, here you were on the floor."

I cleared my throat in an attempt to regain my composure.

"I stubbed my toe on the bastard bed, went flying, and hit my head on the bastard chair. I don't think the furniture likes me."

"You okay?" She chuckled. "I think you'll live. Not sure about the bed and chair."

I laughed, but when I did, my head hurt a little. I thought grimly about what might have been. Now, the only throbbing was in my little toe and not-so-little forehead.

Sat on the bed, sore, injured, and defeated, I contemplated the failed weekend. At every turn, events had conspired against me. I considered giving up. I was fairly certain Sally liked me, but I didn't think I'd done enough to woo her. This had been no trip to Barcelona.

Catching sight of the table, I gawped. It was laden with enormous bags of sweets, the contents of which were tumbling out of the top. More flashbacks played in my head: the sweets grab, arguing with the couple, trying to persuade the DJ to play that record, and after all that, being thrown out of the wedding.

I'm too old for this, I thought. I'd been in a continual midlife crisis since my mid-thirties. I had a decent, fulfilling, well-paid job. I had loving connections with my family and my sons and a few friendships, but I'd never been able to crack everything at the same time. When my relationships were fantastic, my work would be crap. There was always something not working in my life, and it made me feel lost.

Where was I going to end up? Wedding crashing? That was a new low for me. I shook my head. It was wrong. Not the man I wanted to be. That was it. The final straw. *No more going along with what Sally or anyone else wants.* It was time to do what I wanted and to be my own man.

Yes, I wanted to find someone to settle down with, to bring stability into my life. Single, I was a piece of flotsam bobbing away on stormy waters. I wanted the love, care, and affection that a relationship brought. But I needed to do it on my own terms. I couldn't bank everything on Sally.

I'd been trying too hard to be the man she wanted me to be. I needed to be the man I wanted to be. I'd said exactly the same thing to myself yesterday, but the events of the previous night had shown me I hadn't learned the lesson quite yet. Time to implement real change this time. I remembered seeing myself in the mirror at the party, remembered the shame I'd felt.

I needed to change. If that won Sally over, then so be it. If not, then so be it.

As Sally showered, I leafed through a few tourist brochures, including one for a place called Broadstairs. Hang on a minute that was the other place the waiter had recommended, for older people like me. I scowled at the memory and his remarks. I googled it all the same. *Hmmm, not too far away.* I liked the look of it. Maybe Broadstairs would do for me what Margate and Ramsgate had not. I could only hope.

"Hey, Sally," I said, as she emerged from the bathroom, "shall we call into Broadstairs on the way back?"

"Broadstairs?"

"Yeah, a classy little place. A lot classier than Margate and Ramsgate."

She frowned slightly. "I need to get back for Harry."

"We'll still get back in plenty of time. I want to go. Looks sophisticated."

I could tell I'd piqued her interest. "How far from here?" she asked.

"Less than ten minutes in a car."

She agreed and relief coursed through me. I'd gambled a little and it had worked. Today was my day.

* * *

Under an overcast sky, we wandered around the quiet town, taking in its narrow, steep cobbled streets. I worried about Sally tripping but then reminded myself that after the morning's incident, I should be more concerned about me.

Despite the pep talk I'd given myself, John still loomed in the back of my mind. I imagined him smirking about his impending victory. I studied Sally's face for clues about how she was feeling about me and found none. So I searched for clues elsewhere. Good sign: she linked her arm in mine and got close. Bad sign: the conversation was sparse and didn't expand beyond small talk about the weather and our conflicting views on imminent rain—she thought the rain was coming; I didn't.

I couldn't figure out a way through the impasse. This felt like two old friends meeting up for a walk and a catch-up. I wanted romance, intimacy, and to move our relationship forward.

"Wow, a proper butcher's shop." She pointed to the quaint buildings as we passed. "Oh, and a baker's." I tried but couldn't muster up the same level of excitement for the everyday shops. Then, as we neared the seafront, she stopped and clapped her hands. "Oh my god, an old-fashioned picture house."

I grinned. "I love them. We should go to one sometime." Now, this was a building I could get excited about. I loved the entire experience of going to the cinema. Here was a point of connection, a shared interest, a conversation I could feel comfortable and alive in.

She nodded enthusiastically. "We should snuggle up with popcorn and watch a black-and-white film."

"Yeah, like *It's a Wonderful Life* at Christmas time. That would be amazing."

"Oh, I adore that film. What about you?"

"One of my favourite films ever."

"Really? My ex hated it and used to take the piss out of me for loving it."

Incredulous, I felt a surge of anger towards a bloke I'd never met. He'd hurt Sally, and for what? Liking what I considered to be one of the most beautiful, emotional, and heart-warming films ever. I watched it every Christmas and cried every time too. It was a small insight into her marriage that saddened me. "Why?"

"Because he was a dick. What I ever saw in him I'll never know."

What had she seen in him? It worried me, but then, I'd made poor choices before. I couldn't fault her for that; I'd be a hypocrite. "We all make mistakes. But what a film." I stopped, put my hands on her arms, and pulled her in and hugged her. "We'll watch it together one day and I won't skit at you and we can laugh and cry together."

"Oh my god, you cry at it too?" She cocked her head, smiled, and then kissed my cheek. "You're so not like my ex. That's a good thing."

Feeling my insides warm, I smiled and took her hand. Thank the lord our conversation had moved beyond the weather. I was revelling in the emotional intimacy, and proud of myself for admitting that the film brought me to tears. The idea that one person can make a difference to so many lives moved me. I wanted to have a similar effect on others. Oh and we'd found a film we both loved together, I thought we were destined to have completely different tastes in films. A sure sign we were meant to be. My stomach tingled.

We continued walking and soon passed Charles Dickens' Bleak House, which was now a museum.

"Why all the references to Charles Dickens here?" Sally asked.

"He often holidayed in Broadstairs, and he wrote some of his famous novels here."

"No way, did he? Aw, you are so clever, aren't you? I like that about you." She gazed at me. "How do you know stuff like this?"

"I read about this town before we came here. I love to

research the places I visit. Deepens the connection and enjoyment of the place." I held Sally's gaze. "Do you? Like me?"

"Yes. You're intelligent and I like that."

Beaming inside, I ushered Sally along a street overlooking a park and the sea. The place was working its magic, and I hoped it would continue to. "Shall we stop for an ice cream?" I asked, seeing that we were outside an authentic parlour.

"Oh, darling, I love it. So original, and like a proper old-fashioned one."

I guided her inside with a smile, and we sat down next to each other in a corner booth with red leather seats and a white Formica table. Hmm. Private and intimate. In the centre of the table was a menu. I passed one to Sally. "What are you going to have?" I asked as we perused the choices. "I'm thinking of the coffee and caramel combo. Two scoops."

"Good, don't want a fat belly, do you?" She patted my stomach.

I self-consciously breathed in and pulled my belly in. I touched it under the table and felt the flabbiness. I used to be skinny, with a flat tummy. I disliked my older body and yearned for the firmness of my youth. "I'm getting a two-scoop for me, not because you're telling me. What about you?"

"Oh, okay, touchy." She turned back to the menu. "Something fruity, I think. You should have—Oh, I forgot, you don't eat fruit, do you? I think you should. Healthy for you. Would you do that for me?"

Things were going well. This was no time to back down, despite my feelings about my middle-aged spread.

"No."

"Oh. We'll see." Sally half-smiled.

"Yes, we will." I gave her a half-smile in return.

As we enjoyed our ice cream, I could feel her thigh against mine. The coldness of the ice cream contrasted the hot sexual tension between us. Detouring to Broadstairs had been worth it just for this—the ice cream plus the chemistry equalled pure bliss.

Afterwards, we stopped at a nearby coffee shop and sat outside. I ordered two coffees, and we sipped them while observing dog walkers and tourists. "So what do you think of Broadstairs?" I asked.

"I love it. Has a Victorian feel to it." She gazed towards the sea. "That view is beautiful."

"Much better than Margate, heh?"

"Oh yeah, this is my type of place. Classy. Lovely boutique shops."

"What, more than Ramsgate too?"

Sally smiled the biggest smile of the trip, and I allowed myself a sly grin. At last, I felt the closeness and intimacy with Sally I'd been seeking the whole trip. My mind kept returning to the chemistry between us in the ice-cream parlour, sending up butterflies in my stomach. I couldn't blow it now.

I had to make my move and seal the deal.

6

GIVE LIZ TAYLOR A RUN FOR HER MONEY

After parking outside Sally's house, I walked her to her front door.

"Thank you for the weekend," Sally said. "I know you tried your best, and I made a massive fuss about it not being Barcelona, but I want us to work, and for you to understand me and my needs."

"Me too," I said, trying to sound confident despite my nerves getting the best of me again. "And I think I do get you. You're classy and sophisticated and that's what you want us to be. What I want, too." I so wanted Sally and me to work. The weekend, for all its faults, had solidified this.

"Yes, not too much to ask for. Is it?"

"No. Not at all."

"Thank you, darling."

"And thank you."

I watched as she opened her front door and dumped her coat and bags at the bottom of the stairs. I turned to walk away, still trying desperately to build up my courage. I'd hoped for Sally to ask me in. That hadn't happened. I had to take control.

I took a deep breath and turned around. "Harry's not back for a few hours yet," I said.

Sally smiled. "Two hours."

My smile broadened. "Well, are you going to invite me in or what?" I fingered the magic blue pill in my pocket.

She began climbing the stairs in her house and looked over her shoulder. "You coming up?" I stared at her, momentarily unable to speak. "Don't make me ask twice," she said.

"I'm coming! I'M COMING!"

* * *

"So, what do you reckon?" I asked, staring up at the ceiling. The pill had done its job, and all had gone fantastically well. The doctor had been right after all. Don't mix it with alcohol. One worry gone. My chief concern now was making her my girlfriend. Time to get John out of the picture once and for all. Harry would be back in thirty minutes. I knew if I didn't ask, I would regret it. I took one last deep breath and rolled over onto my left side to face Sally. "Will you be my girlfriend?"

Sally smiled, fluttered her eyelashes, and stroked the side of my face. "Today was just what I needed. I love the braver you. You understand me. I like this you."

"Is that a yes?"

"Yes. But you're on probation. For a start, I'll want better holidays than Margate for a weekend, something more exotic, and classier."

I laughed. She didn't laugh. But she'd said yes. Feeling jubilant, I took Sally's hand and then kissed her, and she kissed me back.

As we pulled away, she cocked her head, grinned, and said, "Hmm, husband number four?"

"Fucking hell, Sally," I said, laughing again. "You would give Liz Taylor a run for her money."

She frowned.

Shit, I thought.

"We all make mistakes, darling, you included." But then she smirked and said with a wink, "We should start thinking about a holiday to the Caribbean."

I smiled, but a blaring thought sounded in my head: *What the hell have I gotten myself into here?* Still, the optimist inside me said, *Everything will be okay now. You got the girl by being brave.*

In wooing Sally, I'd tried to be someone else—classic me. Why be myself when I could be whatever the woman in my life wanted me to be? But she'd chosen me when I relaxed into myself. Thank God. Trying to be someone else was tiring.

The weekend had ended up being less about winning the girl at any cost and more about becoming me. I felt as if I'd begun a journey to discovering who I was and what I wanted. I was looking forward to spending more time being Kevin.

Who knew what might happen next. I had many questions. Had I truly beaten John? Would I relax into the relationship with Sally? Would the braver me last? Where would our travels take us next? Married three times already—should I be worried?

THE NEXT BOOK IN THE SERIES AND A FREE BOOK

Well done you made it right to the end. Thank you for taking a chance on me (sounds a bit like a cheesy love song). You're an amazing human being.

Building a relationship with my readers is the best thing about writing. Join my VIP Readers Club for information on new books and deals plus a free copy of this book as an ebook. The exclusive, prequel book to the Midlife Misadventures series.

Just visit www.kevinjdkelly.com

You can buy non-ebook versions of this book at:

www.amazon.co.uk/dp/B08P8SJB9T

www.amazon.com/dp/B08P8SJB9T

Don't you just love the feel, and the feel of a real book?

You can also pre-order/buy *Midlife Misadventures in Cuba* the first book in the series and see what happened next in my life.

www.amazon.co.uk/dp/B08RP9QC2G

www.amazon.com/dp/B08RP9QC2G

Had I truly beaten John? Would I relax into the relationship with Sally? Would the braver me last? Where would our travels take us next? Married three times already—should I be worried?

Their love life is failing. Will an adventurous vacation explode in chaos, or bring them closer together.

London, England, Kevin Kelly is desperate to save his waning relationship with his girlfriend. Disheartened by numerous splits and reconciliations, she gives him an ultimatum. So, despite his friends warnings, he jets off to Cuba on a mission of romantic salvation.

Unable to speak the language, the couple suffers a string of calamitous mishaps that only increase their already fraught relationship. But just when Kevin finally believes things are improving, he catches her dancing flirtatiously with a nightclub singer.

Can their future survive a hectic holiday as Kevin discovers the truth to happiness.

Written as both an open-hearted travel memoir and a trek to self-realisation. This intriguing tale takes you on an extraordinary journey of love and heartbreak that will make you cry and laugh out loud. Set among the backdrop of fascinating locations like Marrakesh and Cuba, Kevin shares a daring and humorous ride towards his own enlightenment.

Midlife Misadventures in Cuba is the first book in the poignant Trips, Travels and Tales series. If you like raw emotional expeditions, light and dark humour, and excursions to exotic locales, then you'll adore Kevin Kelly's engaging story.

Buy Midlife Misadventures in Cuba, so you can roam the world for meaning!

www.amazon.co.uk/dp/B08RP9QC2G
www.amazon.com/dp/B08RP9QC2G

If you want to see where I hang out social media visit me at my facebook group, facebook.com/MidLifeMisadventurer Or meet me and other awesome memoir book readers and authors at facebook.com/groups/welovememoirs The friendliest group on facebook.

facebook.com/MidLifeMisadventurer

ENJOY THIS BOOK? YOU CAN MAKE A DIFFERENCE

Reviews are the most powerful tools in my arsenal, look at me being all militaristic, but seriously, they help when it comes to getting attention for my books, and the feedback also helps me develop my writing skills.

That's where you come in. Yes, you! The reader. Honest reviews of my books help bring them to the attention of other readers.

If you enjoyed this book I would be grateful if you could spend just a minute or so to rate it and write a review (it can be as short as you like). Thank you very much.

Click the link to jump straight to the Amazon review page:

https://www.tinyurl.com/y6kxv64l

COPYRIGHT

DISCLAIMER

This book is a combination of facts about my life and certain embellishments. I value my crooked smile—that's why I've changed the names of everyone in this book except me, and some characters are an amalgamation of more than one person. Oh, except Mum and Dad. They're called Mum and Dad. Together they created me and my crooked smile, so I know they value both. Not that they're mentioned in this book, except here. But they will be in my next one. I've also taken the liberty to change, invent and alter dates, places, events and details for literary effect. I've also shuffled events around, otherwise my life would look more chaotic than it does in this book. Finally, you should not consider this book anything other than a work of literature. I have a vivid imagination, but a terrible memory.

ACKNOWLEDGMENTS

A huge thank you to everyone who has ever encouraged me to write this book. It's all your fault.

To Rachel Small for her patience and ninja editing skills that helped to turn my ramblings and musing into sentences, paragraphs and chapters.

To 100covers for translating my unconnected brain farts into a coherent cover.

To L for your love and support and for putting up with my artistic outbursts.

Finally to you, the reader, for taking the time to read my books. Long may it continue.

www.ingramcontent.com/pod-product-compliance
Lightning Source LLC
Chambersburg PA
CBHW030920080726
47818CB00032BA/360/J

* 9 7 8 1 8 3 8 3 6 2 2 1 8 *